Charl

I love you guys,

Adolfo

For God alone my
soul waits in silence…
Ps 62:1-2

ALSO BY ADOLFO QUEZADA

A Desert Place
Wholeness: The Legacy of Jesus
Goodbye, My Son, Hello
Walking With God
Loving Yourself for God's Sake
Through the Darkness
Heart Peace
Rising from the Ashes
Sabbath Moments
Radical Love
Compassionate Awareness
Transcending Illness
The Teachings of Jesus
Of Mind and Spirit
A Grief Revisited
Old Soul, Young Spirit
Praying to an Unknown God
Before the Night Comes
Love is My Religion

Return to Silence

Return to Silence

Listen for the Whisper of God

Adolfo Quezada

For those yearning
for the peace of silence.

Contents

Prologue

Perfect silence alone proclaims God.
Maximus the Confessor

Return to Silence: Listen for the Whisper of God was a difficult book for me to write because, although I encourage others to return to silence, it has not always been easy for me to do so. Silence has been an elusive butterfly for me throughout my life; and even now, I sometimes find myself attempting to enter silence by force. But silence cannot be forced, manipulated, controlled, or captured. It is like the vastness of the heavens and the depth of the oceans. Silence holds us, we do not hold silence.

We can prepare ourselves to be quiet and still; and we can make ourselves available and receptive; but, ultimately, deep silence comes to us as grace and cannot be earned or deserved. In fact, it is the opposite of effort and technique. Though we cannot take silence by storm, it is the universal banquet to which we are all invited.

Silence invites us to depth.
Joan Chittister

Silence is more than the absence of sound; it is the presence of consciousness.

A mother asks for silence so that her children may sleep; but in the context of this book, we are asked for silence so that we may come awake, aware of our surroundings, and conscious of God.

I have been drawn to silence ever since I realized the beneficial effects it has had on my well-being. It has given me respite from my noisy life; and it has calmed my emotions and settled my thoughts.

Silence has been my refuge and my place of rest. In more recent times, however, I have experienced silence in a different manner. As I have changed, my relationship with silence has changed. I still benefit from the effects it has on me, but they are no longer my primary motivation for returning to silence.

Whereas in the past, I turned to silence to suckle and nestle me whenever I was under stress and overwhelmed by the hardships of life; I now turn to silence for ecstasy. No, I don't mean the bliss or the rapturous delight or emotional exaltation that the dictionary uses to define ecstasy. Rather, I mean the sense that I experience of being taken out of myself; which is also a definition that the dictionary cites for ecstasy. In silence, my ego fades into the background while my true self moves into the foreground. In silence, I am emptied of my selfish desires and filled with love and compassion for all beings. In silence, it is no longer about me and about my spirituality; rather, it is about listening with all my heart to God's volition. It is about dying into God in full communion.

Paradoxically, even as silence brings me into communion with God, it also decreases my need to talk about God. It seems that the oneness with God that I experience in silence is harder and harder to put into words. In addition, it seems ironic for me to be using words to comment about silence. After all, words, whether written or pronounced are not silence.

> *When I pronounce the word*
> *"silence," I destroy it.*
> Wislawa Szymborska

Nevertheless, this book does include words in the form of my reflections on silence. Next to my reflections I have placed the words of past and present spiritual seekers who have also commented on silence.

My hope is that the contents, format, and brevity of this book will serve as a reminder to you to return to silence and to listen for the whisper of God.

Introduction

*Let us be silent, that we may
hear the whisper of God.*
Ralph Waldo Emerson

Why a whisper? Why not an earthquake, why not a fire? Why does God speak to us in silence?

Perhaps it is because, while blare and uproar may get our attention, such loudness usually prompts fear and anxiety. Being frightened or alarmed instinctively makes us want to fight or flee, not to stop and listen. A whisper that emanates from silence, on the other hand, not only gets our attention, but compels us to listen intently to what is being said. Silence couches a whisper in tender intimacy.

The whisper of God comes to us in different ways. Sometimes it is through our intuition; sometimes it is through the written or spoken words of another; and sometimes it is through the astonishing beauty of nature. Also, if we listen intently during our meditation and allow silence to permeate our body and soul, we may hear the whisper of God. It won't necessarily be in the form of words or audible utterances; it is more likely to manifest as a silent knowing in our heart, or a general sense of direction that we trust indubitably.

Some of us anticipate that the voice of God will be accompanied by heavenly trumpets, burning bushes, or other extraordinary, supernatural signs. But the contrary is true. The voice of

God comes to us in ordinary circumstances and in natural ways. There is no fanfare or parting of the clouds; there is just a small, still voice, a whisper, or just sheer silence. Although the whisper of God is framed in silence, it is not shrouded in mystery; rather, it is clear, simple, and grounded in the ordinariness of everyday life.

> *The true contemplative…waits on*
> *the word of God in silence,*
> *and, when he is answered it is not so*
> *much by a word that bursts*
> *into his silence. It is by his silence*
> *itself, suddenly, inexplicably*
> *revealing itself to him as a word of*
> *great power, full of the voice of God.*
> Thomas Merton

Eventually, we come to realize that, like the incessant silence that surrounds us, the whisper of God is forever with us. God is always speaking to our heart, but, unfortunately, we are not always listening.

To listen for the whisper of God continuously is to live a God-conscious life. We live mindfully, that is, more aware of what is happening in the moment before us; and we listen attentively to hear what God requires of us.

HOW TO READ THIS BOOK

This book is not meant to be read straight through; rather, it is to be read slowly, taking time to reflect on each entry. It is written in short, poignant, nonsequential paragraphs that offer my personal perspective about silence.

Next to my reflections are quotations about silence by past and present spiritual seekers. The reflections and the quotations were chosen to complement each other and are meant to be read together.

Sheer Silence

Now there was a great wind, so strong that it was splitting mountains and breaking rocks in pieces before the Lord, but the Lord was not in the wind; and after the wind an earthquake, but the Lord was not in the earthquake; and after the earthquake a fire, but the Lord was not in the fire; and after the fire a sound of sheer silence.

1 Kings 19:11-13

Our purpose for seeking silence is more important than our zealous and impassioned effort to find it. If what we wish to acquire through silence is rest and relaxation, healing and restoration, wholeness and enlightenment, peace and well-being; then the gate that leads to the realm of silence will be closed to us. Silence is simply the means toward our ultimate end - to be at one with God.

Here, in the silence, is where Spirit speaks to me in an inaudible language that my whole self: mind, body, spirit, understands. In the silence, the inner realization of God's presence, I find guidance and confidence to make decisions. I feel oneness with God.

Daily Word

Silence has more to do with our spirit than it does with our mind. Our return to silence is not a case of mind over matter; rather, it is an act of spiritual surrender. Willpower has no role when it comes to silence. Instead, what matters is waiting receptively and attentively; as we listen for the whisper of God.

Listen to the silence

and you hear the soul.

Jernej Graj

We are like fish in water, seeking water. But silence is within us; we need not seek it elsewhere. We have only to turn within to find it.

The central silence is the purest element of the soul's exalted place, the core, the essence of the soul.

Meister Eckhart

We enter into silent meditation, not to reflect on ourselves, but to forget ourselves. In silence we let go of self-consciousness, self-importance, and self-aggrandizement. Silence asks us to leave our ego-driven energy behind and to enter naked, open, and vulnerable.

*Meditation is the journey from
sound to silence, from a limited
identity to unlimited space.*

Sri Sri Ravi Shankar

Sometimes we can sit for long periods of time in meditation and not experience even a hint of silence. Other times, we may be carrying on the normal business of the day when suddenly we are surprised by silence in the most unexpected way and the least likely circumstances. This is the way of silence; it gives itself to us, not as a way to negotiate life, but as life itself.

I've begun to realize that you can listen to silence and learn from it. It has a quality and a dimension all its own.

Chaim Potok

Silence is not our escape into blissful ecstasy. On the contrary, it is the canvass on which our human suffering has been painted with the sweat and blood of our body and soul. It is our wounded heart that gives profundity to our silence. Silence is the sum of all that is our human life, including our afflictions. Yet, we find peace in silence even as we listen for the whisper of God.

A day of silence can be

a pilgrimage in itself.

Hafez

Sometimes we deliberately invite silence to envelop us through meditation, but often silence visits us without notice or invitation. Silence is like a hummingbird that lights on a branch near us to remind us to *break* from our busyness, to *breathe* the breath of God, and to *be* silent.

True silence is the rest of the mind, and it is
to the spirit what sleep is to the body,
nourishment and refreshment.

William Penn

Even as we recognize the benefits of silence, we are in awe of our God-given ability to communicate verbally with one another. We cherish our voice, just as we do the silence from which it emanates.

It would be inhuman for men if they should always keep silence and never be allowed to speak.

Hildegaard

Sometimes the vicissitudes of life overwhelm us and we are filled with fear, anxiety, anger or depression; and we are rendered incapacitated. Although silence has no magic power to rid us of negative emotions, it does clear our mind and heart enabling us to discern and decide how best to confront our problems. Silence leads us to the core of our being where we rediscover the best of ourselves.

In the attitude of silence the soul
finds the path in a clearer light...

Mahatma Gandhi

We live in tumultuous times; and we are stressed by the tension in the air. Loudness masquerades as importance; and clamor demands our attention. We are wont to enter silence to pacify our soul.

Go placidly amid noise and haste,
and remember what peace there may be in
silence.

Desiderata

23

We serve others by bringing silence into the world. We *are* silence in the midst of a noisy, chaotic world. We set aside all else and bestow to others the gift of conscious listening.

The word listen contains the same

letters as the word for silent.

Alfred Brendel

Sound is contingent on a listening ear; silence is as well. So if we are to know silence we must first be listeners. In fact, silence comes to us, not because we have eliminated sound, but because we have listened attentively.

Listen to the wind, it talks.
Listen to the silence, it speaks.
Listen to your heart, it knows.

        Native American Proverb

Our mind is noisy, even when we are praying to God. So we allow our mind to rest while we listen for the whisper of God. It speaks of love and harmony; it offers respite and release.

Souls of prayer are
souls of great silence.

Mother Teresa

We return to silence often through the day. Whatever the circumstances before us, it is always time to enter into silence. Nothing else affects us as silence does. But silence will not open to us until we stop what we are doing, tend to our breathing, and drop the shield that guards our heart.

Let silence take you
to the core of life.
Rumi

We tell ourselves that our silent time is special. We seek out a place to center down and enter into prayer. But there are people in our midst; the room we're in is not a sacred space; the noise outside is loud; there's just too much distraction here. So we move on in search of yet another place where we can be alone with God.

There is no need to go to India or anywhere else to find peace.

You will find that deep place of silence right in your room, your garden, or even your bathtub.

Elizabeth Kubler-Ross

We have been graced with a voice with which to speak out against injustice; and we have received the gift of silence with which to commune with God.

For everything there is a season, and a time for every matter under heaven...a time to keep silence, and a time to speak.

Eccl 3:1, 7

Sometimes in our desperation we pray, begging for solutions to our problems, and pleading for a roadmap to our life. Yet, no answers come; no diagrams are offered. We are left to our own devices.

The inspiration you seek is already within you. Be silent and listen.

Rumi

We silence the memories, the worries, the fantasies, and the wayward ventures of our mind; not by chasing them away, but by listening for silence and paying attention to the spaces between our distractions. The rest just fades away.

Who are you in the silence
between your thoughts?

Gil Fronsdal

We live in fear of what could happen to us and to our loved ones. What if we get sick? What if we lose our job or are forced to incur great debt? What if the cost of living goes up? What if our investments go down? What if…what if…

Move outside the tangle of
fear-living. Live in silence.

Rumi

In silence, our memory is held in abeyance. This does not rob us of our personal identity; rather, it gives us a glimpse of our true identity. In silence, our imagination is suspended temporarily. This does not affect our creativity nor our ability to dream of what can be; rather, it compels us to face the reality that is before us. In silence, our fears and anxieties are put on hold. This does not liberate us from our concerns; rather, it teaches us to confront our problems with the wisdom and equanimity with which we are graced by silence.

Like still water that reflects things as they are, the calming silence helps us to see things more clearly and therefore, to be in deeper contact with ourselves and those around us.

Thich Nhat Hanh

We enter into silent meditation with no expectation or agenda; but we shouldn't be surprised when, beyond our thoughts, emotions, and concepts; we experience enhanced awareness – the gift of silence.

Meditation is silence. If you realize that you really know nothing, then you will be truly meditating. Such truthfulness is the right soil for silence. Silence is meditation.

Yogaswami

To hear the voice of God we need to come away from the madding crowd to a place of solitude and silence. Sometimes, however, to hear the voice of God we need to go *into* the crowd to listen to the voices of the poor, the sick, and the neglected of the world. Theirs is the voice of God.

Perhaps the most important thing we bring to another person is the silence in us, not the sort of silence that is filled with unspoken criticism or hard withdrawal. The sort of silence that is a place of refuge, of rest, of acceptance of someone as they are.

Rachel Reman

In silence we listen for the whisper of God. It comes to us as we are walking on a secluded desert trail or sitting in the quiet of an empty church. It comes to us as we are reading from sacred writings or listening to the dove's morning song. It comes to us because we are listening with all our heart.

The voice of God is heard
only in the depth of silence.

Baba

As we recollect our mind, we are aware of the myriad thoughts, worries, and distractions that scatter our attention, and we let them be. All on their own they pass into oblivion. We return to conscious breathing, ready to receive the peace of silence.

Just as silent currents underlie all the
surface waves of an ocean, the silent depths
of the mind support all our conscious mental
activity.

Harold H. Bloomfield, M.D.

We may be at odds with those who live life differently than we do, with those whose views we do not understand, and with those whose spirit has called them to a realm with which we're unfamiliar. Perhaps our differences will never be reconciled, and that's all right. But we know that there is something we share in common with everyone, and that is silence. In the depth of silence we will always find accord.

If I could prescribe just one remedy
for all the ills of the modern world, I would
prescribe silence. For even if the word of God
was proclaimed in the modern world, no one
would hear it; there is too much noise.
Therefore, create silence.

Kierkegaard

Our investment in external endeavors returns great dividends, yet, our life needs so much more. It needs us to return to internal silence often through the day. Silence is the page upon which we write our life one moment at a time.

Only the inner silence is yours.

No one gave it to you. You were born

with it and you will die with it. Thoughts

have been given to you. You have been

conditioned to them.

Osho

Silence is the fountain of goodness. Yet, it can also be used as a weapon of iniquity. There are those who choose to punish others with whom they are in conflict by giving them the "silent treatment" instead of talking with them in the hope of resolving their differences. There are also those whose cowardice keeps them from speaking out against injustice. They believe their silence is more prudent than their protest. Malefactors act with impunity when good people remain silent.

I swore never to be silent whenever and wherever human beings endure suffering and humiliation.

Elie Wiesel

In silence, the resentments we hold against others fall away from our heart. Silence holds on to nothing; it is the ultimate forgiveness.

Blessed are the merciful,
for they will receive mercy.

Mt 5:7

Inevitably, one day we will be invited into the ultimate silence. It is for this day that we have prepared. That day will be a day of joy and sorrow, gain and loss. There will be weeping and laughing, and there will be silence.

Returning to the source is silence,

which is the way of nature.

Lao Tsu

We need not be afraid of silence. While it is true that silence will expose us to our woundedness, it will also help us to accept it, embrace it, and perhaps to heal it.

The eternal silence of these
infinite spaces fills me with dread.

Blaise Pascal

Silence is a trek into the desert where our mind becomes barren and our spirit profuse. Silence is the darkness of the night that forces us to wait with patience for the coming of the dawn.

I will lead her into the desert,
and speak to her heart.
Hosea 2:14

Our return to silence is a little death that leaves us stripped to the soul. In silence, the mundane and the profane disappear; and the superfluous falls away. Silence sanctifies us; and we are made whole.

Silence bears the wholeness

we keep looking for.

Robert Sardello

Living in silence does not mean that we must enter a cloistered monastery and hold our tongue forever more. It simply means that we are careful with our words lest we do harm with them. It means that we avoid idle talk, gossip, and other negative conversation. It means that we respect the right of others, and minimize the noise we make.

Before you speak ask yourself: Is it kind? Is it true? Is it necessary? Does it improve upon the silence?

Shirdi Sai Baba

We do not have to police our mind to stop the flow of extraneous thoughts. Just paying close attention to the mother hummingbird nesting outside our window automatically drops all thoughts from our mind. Listening to the children playing in the school yard relegates all other noises to the background. Silent living is conscious living, and conscious living is fulfilled living.

Since I have learned to be silent,

everything has come so much closer

to me.

Rainer Maria Rilke

Returning to silence is not just a technique that we learn and then practice. Rather, it is a rediscovery of our human ability to clear our mind of the thoughts and emotions that impede living consciously in the present moment, and listening for the whisper of God.

*It is only when the mind is brought
into silence, into full presence within this
moment, in the here and now; that you will
ever be truly free.*

Marcus T. Anthony

Strong cravings and powerful temptations come upon us with unexpected speed and great ferocity, and can easily overtake our defenses. But even these mighty foes are no match for our inner silence because, in silence, they have nothing to which to cling. Cravings and temptations simply go away until another day.

In silence, man can most readily

preserve his integrity.

Meister Eckhart

In silence, our will is made one with the will of God. This does not mean that our will is taken from us; rather, it is we who set down our will and take up the will of God as it is revealed to us. God's will becomes our will and we abide by it forever.

In the silence of
the heart God speaks.
Mother Teresa

Sometimes existence is painful and overwhelming, and the troubles of life bring us low. Yet, even in our woundedness we know to return to silent meditation. Silence does not take away our pain or deny our vulnerability; instead, it holds our pain and shares our grief. Above all, silence clears our path of mental and emotional hindrances so that we may focus on the challenge before us.

Meditation is not passive sitting in silence. It is sitting in awareness, free from distraction, and realizing the clear understanding that arises from concentration.

Thich Nhat Hanh

Try as we may, our mind cannot commune with God through thoughts and concepts. Our heart, however, enters into communion with God through profound silence and the intimacy of one.

The noblest attainment in this life is to be silent and let God work and speak within.

Meister Eckhart

Silence is not an extraordinary phenomenon known only to an elite group of spiritually-gifted individuals. It is a common, ordinary, everyday reality that is available to anyone who is willing to be open and available to it.

*Without everyday life, it is
impossible to experience silence.*

Dainin Katagiri

We need not be concerned that living in silence we will change our basic self. On the contrary, silence compels us to be congruent with our true self.

Silence means you have to be you as you really are – what is, just is of itself.

Dainin Katgiri

We are mind and body, yet our attention is placed predominantly on the thoughts and emotions that emanate from our mind. Little attention, if any, is directed toward our body. Our first step toward silence is to get physically grounded. Our return to silence must include awareness of our body, including conscious breathing and relaxation of our total physical self.

I have grown up amongst the sages
and have found nothing better for the body
than silence.

Pirkei Avos

Noise is not our enemy, not if it prompts us to seek out silence. This is especially true with regard to internal noise. We do not chase away the noises from our mind; instead, we let them be a reminder to us to return to the everlasting realm of silence.

Our noisy years seem moments
in the being of the eternal silence.
William Wordsworth

•

What does silence have to do with God? Simply put, silence is the language of the heart; it is our means of communing with God.

Silence is the language of God,

all else is poor translation.

Rumi

Taking silence into the world with us does not mean that we separate ourselves from the rest of humanity. On the contrary, carrying silence into our daily life helps us to connect with those who are suffering, and to treat them with kindness and compassion. Grounded in silence, our relationships are authentic, selfless, and peaceful.

Silence is a great peacemaker.

Henry Wadsworth Longfellow

Silence purifies our heart by breaking us free from the chains that bind us to the trite and the mundane. It purifies our heart by stripping away the facades we use to impress, and the masks we wear to hide. Silence purifies our heart by taking away our pernicious cravings; and it leaves us with the sole aspiration to be at one with God.

Perfect prayer does not consist in many words, silent remembering and pure intention raises the heart to that supreme Power.

Amit Ray

When we least expect it, silence breaks into the cacophony that pervades our life, and invites us to come away and rest a while.

Where shall the word be found,
where shall the word resound? Not here,
there is not enough silence.

T.S. Eliot

Silence is not contingent on the cessation of external noise. It is not guaranteed by the elimination of dissonance and chaos. We can insert earplugs and close ourselves off in a sound-proof chamber and yet not know silence because of the internal commotion and disturbance that continues in our mind. Conversely, we may find ourselves in the middle of a sports arena with an exuberantly loud and tumultuous crowd and still experience silence within ourselves. Ultimately, silence is in the internal ear of the listener.

There are times when silence

has the loudest voice.

Leroy Brownlow

To truly listen to another we must first silence our mind and open our heart. Our silence invites divulgence, while our heart offers itself as a safe and confidential receiver. Silence enables us to hear the weeping of a wounded soul, the laughter of a child, the sweet words of a poet, and the whisper of God.

When someone is going through a storm, your silent presence is more powerful than a million empty words.

Thelma Davis

Our ability to speak is a wonderful gift, as anyone who has lost their ability to communicate verbally will attest. As with any gift, however, we must use our gift of speech wisely, lovingly, and sparingly. We speak when we believe that what we have to say is more important than not speaking. Otherwise, we choose silence.

Be silent or let your words
be worth more than silence.

Pythagoras

Equal to the peace of silence that lets us rest in God is the loneliness of silence that keeps us strangers to those who pass our way. Let us not bypass one another in a fog of silence; rather, let us stop to greet each other; let us find our common ground.

Ships that pass in the night, and
speak each other in passing,
Only a signal shown and a distant
voice in the darkness;
So in the ocean of life, we pass and
speak one another, only a look and a voice,
then darkness again and a silence.

Our return to silence can come at anytime and in any place, but the merciless noises of the day may compel us to wait until the world is sleeping. Then, in the stillness of the night and the quiet of our mind, we enter our silent reverie.

Then he went out to the mountain to pray, spending the night in communion with God.

Lk 6:12

Should we silence our mind so that we can be attentive or should we be attentive so that we can silence our mind? Neither. It is our humility and receptivity that allow silence to be heard; and it is our love and caring that induces our attention. Deep silence and caring attention are complementary principles of life.

The most important gifts you can give are your love, time, and attention.

Nishan Panwar

Even a little while of silent living restores our soul and animates our spirit. We come away from the realm of silence with renewed vigor and greater appreciation for life.

Silence is a source
of great strength.

Lao Tzu

We put words together and offer them to God in prayer, but they do not seem enough. They do not provide the intimacy for which our heart yearns; and they fall short of the communion for which our soul longs. Then our prayer falls silent. There is no sound except the beating of our heart; there is no thought except for our awareness of God's presence. It is then that pure silence becomes our prayer.

I closed my mouth and spoke
to you in a hundred silent ways.

Rumi

Though we enter the realm of silence, we are not immune from the noises of the world; but we are given the equanimity to withstand and transcend them, while remaining mindful of the now.

When you become aware of silence,
immediately there is that state of inner still
alertness. You are present.

Eckhart Tolle

There are times that call for silence and nothing else will do. To sit in silence in the presence of a grieving friend may be the best thing we can do because, in the midst of great suffering, words get in the way.

Silence is a friend

that never betrays.

Confucius

The word *silence* is a noun, but it is also a verb. We have the ability to silence our thoughts, our memories, our fantasies, our preoccupations, and our projections of the future. No matter where our thoughts may take us, silence transports us back to the present moment when our life is taking place.

Love has no past or future, and so it is with this extraordinary state of silence.

Krishnamurti

How alluring the silence of the desert is where even the still small voice of the emerald hummingbird can be heard, and the heavily flapping wings of the mighty hawk announce its majesty. Without silence nothing can be heard.

The true call of the desert, of the mountains,
or the sea, is their silence – free of the
networks of dead speech.

Freya Stark

Sometimes   silence   is   all   that
comes from God, or so it seems. Try as

we may to make a connection with God, all we get back is silence. Even if all we ask for is a small sign to let us know that we are on the right path, God seems silent. It is easy to lose faith at times like these, unless we consider that the silence of God may be preparing us to face more difficult challenges ahead. Ultimately, what we need from God we already have. God's apparent silence teaches us silence. In our worst of times it is our silence that makes us receptive to the strength, courage, and love that God instills in us. Through all the vicissitudes of our life, the silence of God resounds in our heart.

God's silence is how it feels,

it's not how it is.

Jon Bloom

Silence keeps us honest. Without distractions there is no place to hide. In the midst of silence the naked truth comes knocking on our door, and it will not be denied entry into our life.

Silence is the mother of truth.

Benjamin Disraeli

Jesus craved silence and went into the wilderness to find it. He knew that without letting go of all that filled his mind, he could not listen for the whisper of God. Through silence, Jesus heard the will of God on the hill and descended into the valley to fulfill it.

…Jesus was silent.

Mt 26:63

Deep silence gives us a glimpse of death. It enables us to discern between what we truly need and what we deem superfluous. It helps us distinguish between what's real and what's illusion. Deep silence resembles the sense of nonbeing that may be a part of death. In deep silence there is diminished desire for things material, and a lack of ambition for accomplishments. In deep silence, nothing matters more than love.

Death must be so beautiful. To lie in soft brown earth with the grasses waving above one's head, and listen to silence. To have no yesterday, and no tomorrow. To forget time, to forgive life, to be at peace.

Oscar Wilde

In the midst of silence our capacity to discern is enhanced, while our need to judge is abated. In the midst of silence our desire to know gives way to our acceptance of not knowing; and our insistence on certainty yields to our assent to ambiguity.

Silence is the sleep that

nourishes wisdom.

Francis Bacon

Silence may seem illusive to us in this world of noise and distraction, yet silence is always at our disposal waiting for our return. Silence is the nest on which we light after a long and arduous flight; it is the place to rest our mind and tend our soul. The return to silence is as simple as listening for it, even through the dissonance.

I let the silence drop like a pebble into the middle of my day and send its ripples out over its surface in ever-widening circles.

David Steindl-Rast

When, in the midst of our silent reverie, we hear disturbing noises, we don't have to be distracted; we don't have to be disturbed. Instead, we simply acknowledge the noises and allow them to become a part of our experience; we let them enter into our silence and become absorbed by it.

Learn to be silent. Let your quiet mind listen and absorb the silence.

Pythagoras

When we find ourselves in the actual or metaphorical wilderness of life, we encounter silence whether we are seeking it or not. Actually, it is silence that finds us in the midst of the unknown. Because the wilderness of life is unfamiliar to us, and because it is dangerous and unpredictable, we enter silent prayer and pay single-hearted attention to the whisper of God who guides our way.

Blessed are the single-hearted,

for they will see God.

Mt 5:8

We are born from the womb of silence. Silence is our foundation, our core, our true nature. Of all that we have in common with others, silence is the most basic. At the base of our souls, we are in silent union with all. At the end of our life, we share the oneness of God.

Let silence take you

to the core of life.

Rumi

Thoughts that arise from our reactive emotions, such as fear, anger, despair, envy, or hate, will likely lead us astray. Thoughts that emanate from the silent depths of our heart, however, are more likely to guide us well. When in doubt, we go silent; we listen to the voice of our heart.

The song of the voice is sweet, but the song of the heart is the pure voice of heaven.

Khalil Gibran

We breathe the breath of God; we let it fill our lungs and carry life to every part of our body. We let breath feed our mind and animate our soul. Breath is spirit and spirit is life. As silence envelops our mind, we are free to focus on the object of our choice. We choose life in the form of breath. We place our attention on each inhalation and each exhalation; and thus we attend to the rhythm of our life.

Silence: the breath is precious.

An Old Persian Proverb

To give our attention to that which is most important, we must first take our attention away from that which is less important. We will know which is which by listening to the whisper of God in our heart.

God is whispering in your heart, in the whole existence, just tune your ears.

Amit Ray

We *listen* to the voice of our heart, and we *speak* with the voice of our heart. Words that emanate from deep silence are kind, compassionate, and truthful. Our silent heart is rooted in love and speaks only to affirm, encourage, and heal. Our words are welcome if they are relevant and brief. Our silence too is welcome, especially by those who need to be heard. Sometimes our silence has a greater impact than our words.

A judicious silence is always better
Than truth spoken without charity.

St. Frances de Sales

In the early morning hours we hear the song of doves break into the silence of the dawn. With no apparent conductor to orchestrate their symphony, the birds sing out in praise of the newborn day. But only moments ago they were not singing. There was only silence, the silence that waited patiently to be part of the morning ritual. We listen to the sound, we listen to the silence; what beautiful music they make together.

Music and silence combine strongly
because music is done with silence, and
silence is full of music.

Marcel Marceau

When in silent meditation, there is no reason for us to judge ourselves when our mind becomes distracted. Such judgment becomes just one more distraction. Instead, we welcome the distractions that come and acknowledge their appearance; then we wait as they float into oblivion. We return to conscious breathing and to an even deeper silence than before we were distracted.

Meditation is just courage

to be silent and alone.

Osho

Our return to silence is a return to essence, to the core of existence, to basic being. Here, in silent waiting, self-consciousness falls away and we are left exposed to the elements of heaven: oneness with all that is, universal love, and the lightness of nonbeing.

In the attitude of silence the soul finds the path in a clearer light, and what is elusive and deceptive resolves itself into crystal clearness. Our life is a long and arduous quest after Truth.

Mahatma Gandhi

Silence compels us to face the reality before us. Perhaps that is why some of us are afraid to enter into silence. If we have depended on noisy distractions to keep loneliness at bay; or if we have considered the sound of our voice as proof of life; perhaps it is because we fear that silence may lead to our annihilation. Silence may indeed lead us to stillness, to boundlessness, to vastness, and to the state of unknowning; but the only thing that silence does away with is the internal dissonance that inhibits our ability to listen for the whisper of God.

The truth is known in silence.

Be still and know.

Leonard Jacobson

To return to silence we must listen for silence. Paradoxically, as we listen for silence, we hear so many other sounds. But the space between the sounds is silence, and we can hear it too. Whether in meditation or on a morning walk, myriad sounds come to the foreground of our hearing. Each sound is unique and interesting; and each is beautifully framed in silence. We focus on the sounds one at a time and acknowledge them; then, as if returning home, we return to silence. This is the cycle of conscious living.

It was good to get back and smell the sweet air of the woods and to listen to the silence.

Thomas Merton

We listen to the silence of our heart; it echoes the silence of God. We know God in silence, without images, concepts, pomp, or circumstance. We know God in the darkness of the night and the uncertainty of tomorrow.

Silent is the eloquent expression

of the inexpressible.

Sri Chinmay

We make silence a way of life. There is no time or place that does not provide an opportunity for us to open to the silence that awaits us. We enter into silence as many times as we remember to do so. Once we dare return to silence, we must trust it and let it lure us into the depths where we commune with God.

Above anything, welcome silence, for
it brings fruits that no tongue can speak of,
neither can it be explained.

Isaac of Nineveh

Our yearning for silence is a yearning for God. Nothing resounds like the silence of God. Our silence is not a void, but a vessel waiting to be filled with the love of God.

What we need most in order to make progress is to be silent before this great God with our appetite and with our tongue, for the language he best hears is silent love.

St. John of the Cross

In silence we are not just being quiet; we are listening for the voice of God in our heart. Our intimacy with God is cultivated in silence because it is in silence that we are most authentic. We are summoned into the silence of God, for it is in silence that we are one with God and with all existence.

If we really want to pray we must first listen, for in the silence of the heart God speaks.

T.S. Eliot

While it is true that the silent atmosphere of a chapel is conducive to prayer and meditation, external silence by itself does not open us to the presence of God. Rather, it is our internal silence, regardless of external noise, that allows our heart to hear the whisper of God.

We cannot put ourselves directly in the presence of God if we do not practice internal and external silence.

Mother Teresa

Before all else, there was silence; and when all else has ceased to be, there will be silence. Noise ends; silence is forever.

See the world as it is, small and blue,

beautiful in that eternal silence

where it floats.

Archibald Macleish

Let us hold precious our capacity to keep silence, for only the vastness of silence can encompass the magnitude of our existence; and only the profundity of silence can reveal our oneness with God.

Nothing in all creation
is so like God as silence.

Meister Eckhart

Epilogue

*Deepest communion with God is
beyond words, on the other side of silence.*
Madeleine L'Engle

Blessed are those who seek peace, for they will be graced with silence.

We are all graced with silence. It is an inherent human capacity. It is the gift of respite, and it is the salve that heals our woundedness and promotes our well-being; but silence is so much more to us. It is our lifeline to the essence of our existence.

Eliminating the external noises that disturb us promotes wellness; but it doesn't necessarily bring us the peace for which our soul yearns so desperately. Disciplining ourselves to practice certain breathing techniques, and repeat particular words may go a long way to optimize our physical and mental health; but it doesn't necessarily carry us to the depths of silence to which we are capable of descending; and at which we rendezvous with God.

Quieting down our environment and practicing ways to center ourselves are necessary steps that we take toward deep silence; but our actions can take us only so far. There is a point at which all we can do is surrender ourselves to the mercy of silence. We wait patiently and faithfully for what is to come; and we listen attentively for the whisper of God.

Beyond our doing, and beyond our control, deep silence comes for us, as though it were an angel taking our hand and leading us to the presence of our Beloved, where we abide in intimate communion.

Adolfo Quezada, a retired counselor and psychotherapist, has authored twenty books on psycho-spiritual topics. He holds master's degrees in counseling and in journalism from the University of Arizona. Quezada, who is married and has four children and five grandchildren, lives in Tucson, Arizona.

67149873R00113

Made in the USA
Lexington, KY
03 September 2017